1OOO
patterns

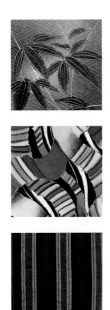

DESIGN *through* THE CENTURIES

1000 patterns

General editor

DRUSILLA COLE

Contributors

**ALAN BRIDGEWATER,
CHRISTINE DAVIS, & IAIN ZACZEK**

CHRONICLE BOOKS

SAN FRANCISCO

First published in the United States in 2003
by CHRONICLE BOOKS LLC

Copyright © 2003 THE IVY PRESS LIMITED
All rights reserved. No part of this book may
be reproduced in any form without written
permission from the publisher.

Library of Congress Cataloging-in-Publication
Data available.

ISBN 0-8118-3979-6

Distributed in Canada by RAINCOAST BOOKS
9050 Shaughnessy Street, Vancouver,
British Columbia V6P 6E5

10 9 8 7 6 5 4 3 2 1

CHRONICLE BOOKS LLC
85 Second Street
San Francisco, California 94105
www.chroniclebooks.com

This book was created by

THE IVY PRESS LTD
The Old Candlemakers,
Lewes, East Sussex BN7 2NZ

CREATIVE DIRECTOR   Peter Bridgewater

PUBLISHER   Sophie Collins

EDITORIAL DIRECTOR   Steve Luck

DESIGN MANAGER   Tony Seddon

DESIGNER   Jane Lanaway

SENIOR PROJECT EDITOR   Caroline Earle

DTP DESIGNER   Chris Lanaway

PICTURE RESEARCHER   Vanessa Fletcher

CONTRIBUTORS   Alan Bridgewater,
Christine Davis, Iain Zaczek

Manufactured in China by Hong Kong Garphics and Printing Ltd.

Contents

Pattern_finder_

The patterns in the pattern finder are categorized by motif and subject matter, as well as being fully cross-referenced with alternative names and terms. There are six categories in the pattern finder: regions/ethnic origin; basic shapes; natural shapes; mythological, religious, and symbolic patterns; artifacts; and named periods/art movements. All the numbering in the pattern finder refers to the pattern numbers only, and not to page numbers.

REGIONS/ETHNIC ORIGIN

CASPIAN REGION 233, 234, 235, 236, 237, 238, 239, 240, 241, 242, 243, 244, 245, 246, 247, 248, 249, 250, 251, 252, 253, 254, 255, 256, 257, 258, 259, 260, 261, 262, 263, 264, 265, 266, 267, 268, 269, 270, 271, 272, 273, 274, 275, 276, 277, 278, 279, 280, 281, 282

CELTIC 446, 447, 448, 449, 450, 451, 452, 453, 454, 455, 456, 457, 458, 459, 460, 461, 462, 463, 464, 899

CHINA 54, 55, 56, 57, 58, 59, 60, 61, 62, 63, 64, 65, 66, 67, 68, 69, 70, 71, 72, 73, 74, 75, 76, 77, 78, 79, 80, 81, 82, 83, 84, 85

CLASSICAL WORLD 283, 284, 285, 286, 287, 288, 289, 290, 291, 292, 293, 294, 295, 296, 297, 298, 299, 300, 301, 302, 303, 304, 305, 306, 307, 308, 309, 310, 311, 312, 313, 314, 315, 316, 317, 318, 319, 320, 321, 322, 323, 324, 325

COLONIAL NORTH AMERICA 433, 434, 435, 436, 437, 438, 439, 440, 441, 442, 443, 444, 445

INDIA & PAKISTAN 143, 144, 145, 146, 147, 148, 149, 150, 151, 152, 153, 154, 155, 156, 157, 158, 159, 160, 161, 162, 163, 164, 165, 166, 167, 168, 169, 170, 171, 172, 173, 174, 175, 176, 177, 178, 179, 180, 181, 182, 183, 184, 185, 186, 187, 188, 189, 190, 191, 192, 193

INDONESIA 24, 25, 26, 27, 28, 29, 30, 31, 32, 33, 34, 35, 36, 37, 38, 39, 40, 41, 42, 43, 44, 45, 46, 47, 48, 49, 50, 51, 52, 53

JAPAN 86, 87, 88, 89, 90, 91, 92, 93, 94, 95, 96, 97, 98, 99, 100, 101, 102, 103, 104, 105, 106, 107, 108, 109, 110, 111, 112, 113, 114, 115, 116, 117, 118, 119, 120, 121, 122, 123, 124, 125, 126, 127, 128, 129, 130, 131, 132, 133, 134, 135, 136, 137, 138, 139, 140, 141, 142

PERSIA 194, 195, 196, 197, 198, 199, 200, 201, 202, 203, 204, 205, 206, 207, 208, 209, 210, 211, 212, 213, 214, 215, 216, 217, 218, 219, 220, 221, 222, 223, 224, 225, 226, 227, 228, 229, 230, 231, 232

POLYNESIA 1, 2, 3, 4, 5, 6, 7, 8, 9, 10, 11, 12, 13, 14, 15, 16, 17, 18, 19, 20, 21, 22, 23

PRE-COLUMBIAN AMERICA 377, 378, 379, 380, 381, 382, 383, 384, 385, 386, 387, 388, 389, 390, 391, 392, 393, 394, 395, 396, 397, 398, 399, 400, 401, 402, 403, 404, 405, 406, 407, 408, 409, 410, 411, 412, 413, 414, 415, 416, 417, 418, 419, 420, 421, 422, 423, 424, 425, 426, 427, 428, 429, 430, 431, 432

SUB-SAHARAN & NORTH AFRICA 326, 327, 328, 329, 330, 331, 332, 333, 334, 335, 336, 337, 338, 339, 340, 341, 342, 343, 344, 345, 346, 347, 348, 349, 350, 351, 352, 353, 354, 355, 356, 357, 358, 359, 360, 361, 362, 363, 364, 365, 366, 367, 368, 369, 370, 371, 372, 373, 374, 375, 376

BASIC AND GEOMETRIC SHAPES

ABSTRACT 819, 840, 846, 847, 851, 856, 867, 875, 890, 894, 902, 904, 914, 915, 931, 932, 936, 938, 942, 958, 959, 967, 968, 970, 972, 973, 975, 976, 982, 990, 994, 997, 998, 999, 1000

ACANTHUS 465, 466, 483, 484, 485, 486, 487, 488, 514, 515, 639

ADLER/EAGLE MOTIF 257, 259

ARABESQUE 229, 521, 522, 523

ARROW/CHEVRON 18, 19, 50, 150, 156, 199, 202, 203, 252, 257, 259, 283, 344, 351, 353, 358, 363, 382, 397, 415, 752, 806, 808, 813, 842, 861, 877

BASKETWEAVE/LATTICE 86, 116, 135, 137, 141, 342, 343, 344, 345, 494, 597, 669, 797, 864, 985

"BEAUTIFUL GARDEN" DESIGN *see MINA-KHANI*

BOTEH/BUTA/PAISLEY/TEARDROP 21, 146, 158, 164, 165, 166, 167, 168, 169, 170, 171, 185, 272, 273, 497, 500, 503, 777, 828, 876, 889, 905, 909, 910, 913, 917, 923, 935, 946, 948, 950, 954, 960, 971, 972, 984

BUTA *see BOTEH*

CELTIC KNOT *see EVERLASTING KNOT*

CHECKERBOARD 1, 3, 9, 20, 101, 182, 256, 333, 362, 363, 415, 462, 481, 573, 744, 794, 860; *see also* **SQUARE**

CHEVRON *see* **ARROW**

CIRCLE/SPOT 9, 34, 39, 58, 68, 73, 88, 103, 104, 108, 117, 124, 126, 137, 143, 149, 150, 155, 160, 161, 162, 164, 169, 173, 178, 180, 181, 182, 189, 190, 221, 228, 238, 247, 250, 254, 255, 260, 261, 262, 263, 264, 265, 281, 283, 284, 285, 287, 289, 290, 291, 293, 294, 302, 304, 305, 307, 308, 311, 312, 313, 314, 315, 316, 317, 318, 319, 322, 323, 325, 327, 359, 363, 366, 367, 368, 371, 372, 373, 374, 375, 377, 396, 399, 400, 401, 402, 433, 435, 440, 443, 445, 446, 450, 451, 452, 453, 456, 457, 459, 460, 461, 463, 466, 468, 469, 470, 471, 472, 473, 474, 476, 477, 478, 482, 487, 493, 496, 499, 505, 506, 507, 508, 510, 511, 515, 519, 520, 523, 526, 527, 530, 531, 532, 533, 534, 535, 536, 537, 538, 547, 554, 557, 558, 559, 569, 574, 579, 582, 583, 584, 585, 586, 596, 600, 602, 603, 612, 616, 618, 624, 627, 635, 642, 644, 646, 647, 650, 652, 656, 658, 661, 664, 665, 666, 668, 672, 673, 674, 683, 685, 688, 689, 690, 691, 696, 699, 705, 710, 711, 712, 713, 718, 724, 727, 728, 729, 731, 732, 736, 739, 741, 742, 743, 746, 747, 748, 750, 752, 753, 754, 755, 756, 760, 761, 763, 764, 765, 767, 770, 771, 772, 773, 774, 776, 777, 778, 782, 784, 785, 786, 789, 791, 793, 794, 795, 796, 797, 798, 799, 801, 802, 809, 812, 814, 815, 818, 819, 820, 825, 826, 829, 830, 838, 842, 845, 851, 862, 867,

870, 873, 875, 878, 881, 882, 890, 892, 896, 899, 901, 903, 906, 908, 909, 910, 912, 919, 920, 921, 922, 924, 925, 930, 940, 941, 942, 947, 949, 953, 962, 963, 964, 967, 971, 977, 994, 996, 997, 998, 999; *see also* **FLOWER**; **ROSETTE**

CRESCENT/SICKLE 99, 260, 714, 815

CROSS/X 43, 129, 132, 147, 148, 170, 203, 249, 277, 278, 280, 286, 318, 320, 324, 325, 327, 340, 344, 360, 366, 381, 382, 384, 386, 388, 389, 390, 392, 393, 404, 418, 427, 443, 446, 476, 478, 479, 505, 506, 598, 752, 763, 803, 839, 840, 861, 895

DIAMOND 13, 17, 41, 42, 43, 45, 48, 62, 85, 92, 96, 100, 101, 106, 115, 126, 129, 148, 150, 152, 154, 156, 174, 182, 183, 184, 190, 219, 223, 234, 237, 240, 243, 244, 245, 248, 249, 252, 258, 262, 265, 268, 269, 270, 274, 277, 278, 279, 282, 283, 285, 286, 293, 323, 324, 325, 346, 348, 353, 354, 355, 356, 360, 362, 368, 369, 371, 375, 381, 386, 388, 389, 392, 394, 395, 408, 415, 416, 417, 418, 419, 420, 421, 422, 423, 435, 437, 438, 445, 469, 470, 476, 481, 486, 487, 494, 505, 506, 509, 510, 526, 531, 538, 539, 540, 541, 542, 551, 569, 570, 579, 580, 598, 605, 709, 775, 783, 813, 897, 899, 911, 947, 987

EAGLE MOTIF *see* **ADLER**

EGG-AND-TONGUE 294, 544

EVERLASTING/CELTIC/MAGIC KNOT 56, 446, 448, 449, 450, 451, 452, 453, 454, 457, 458, 460, 461, 462, 463, 464, 468, 477, 480, 485, 505, 506, 507, 508, 509, 510, 511, 512, 513, 551

FAN 10, 97, 216, 291, 297, 301, 515, 521, 600, 668, 748, 798

FIGURE-EIGHT 22, 418, 493

FLEUR-DE-LIS 246, 482, 509, 510, 511

GOOD LUCK SYMBOL *see* **SWASTIKA**

GREEK KEY 246, 253, 283, 298

GRID 1, 2, 3, 4, 5, 6, 7, 12, 13, 14, 17, 21, 22, 39, 105, 148, 183, 184, 219, 223, 230, 240, 253, 314, 315, 316, 317, 318, 319, 323, 357, 359, 520, 541, 542, 682, 708, 723, 732, 760, 785, 786, 802, 847, 881, 882, 980

GUL/LOZENGE 154, 223, 225, 251, 254, 270, 274, 276, 277, 278, 279, 415, 422, 499

HARSHANG 252, 253

HEART SHAPE 122, 144, 216, 316, 324, 440, 443, 444, 446, 501, 511, 513, 584, 604, 608, 612, 653, 676, 678, 687, 692, 703, 707, 744, 768, 818, 822, 857, 905, 971

BASIC SHAPES (continued)

HERATI 207, 236, 251

HEXAGON 129, 182, 195, 198, 199, 200, 201, 202, 203, 204, 221, 234, 259, 269, 280, 338, 436, 509, 574, 657

KHANCH 194

LATTICE *see* **BASKETWEAVE**

LOZENGE *see* **GUL**

MAGIC KNOT *see* **EVERLASTING KNOT**

MINA-KHANI/"BEAUTIFUL GARDEN" DESIGN 183, 184, 186, 187, 188

OCTAGON 148, 154, 227, 229, 230, 251, 253, 258, 276, 434, 724

PAISLEY *see* **BOTEH**

PARANG RUSAK/DAGGER 46

PENTAGON 762, 764

POTHOOK 243, 247

ROSETTE 68, 102, 109, 116, 117, 125, 138, 143, 148, 163, 181, 184, 189, 219, 220, 227, 228, 229, 230, 232, 284, 287, 289, 290, 291, 306, 310, 374, 414, 433, 443, 474, 496, 536, 550, 586, 598, 600, 603, 624, 628, 632, 658, 664, 711, 743, 755, 905, 913; *see also* **CIRCLE; FLOWER**

SCROLL 91, 120, 125, 226, 234, 246, 256, 262, 263, 283, 295, 297, 308, 310, 313, 315, 316, 317, 319, 324, 406, 446, 456, 457, 459, 491, 514, 515, 516, 521, 522, 523, 536, 537, 546, 548, 550, 554, 557, 558, 559, 561, 563, 673, 946; *see also* **SPIRAL; WAVE**

SICKLE *see* **CRESCENT**

SPIRAL 22, 52, 81, 161, 284, 286, 363, 441, 456, 457, 459, 485, 547, 582, 710, 720, 728, 751, 753, 782, 846, 855, 875, 876; *see also* **SCROLL; WAVE**

SPOT *see* **CIRCLE**

SQUARE 1, 2, 3, 4, 6, 7, 12, 13, 14, 16, 19, 20, 21, 24, 39, 81, 100, 101, 131, 132, 141, 147, 152, 153, 154, 156, 199, 227, 229, 231, 235, 247, 253, 254, 256, 258, 259, 268, 270, 280, 282, 283, 299, 300, 303, 320, 322, 324, 325, 326, 327, 330, 331, 333, 340, 342, 343, 344, 345, 346, 347, 349, 354, 355, 356, 357, 358, 359, 363, 364, 367, 370, 373, 376, 377, 384, 385, 388, 396, 397, 409, 413, 414, 424, 426, 430, 432, 433, 435, 437, 438, 439, 442, 447, 455, 462, 466, 474, 480, 481, 494, 498, 499, 505, 506, 511, 512, 515, 535, 570, 571, 572, 573, 575, 576, 577, 578, 587, 588, 589, 590, 591, 592, 593, 594, 595, 597, 682, 708, 709, 717, 722, 723, 733, 734, 738, 746, 773, 785, 791, 799, 804, 805, 806, 809, 821, 823, 829, 831, 833, 836, 837, 839, 843, 846, 848, 850, 853, 860, 864, 865, 872, 879, 880, 908, 929, 937, 941, 944, 955, 964, 969, 970, 974, 980, 983, 990, 993, 994, 995, 999; *see also* **CHECKERBOARD**

STAR 9, 10, 13, 93, 112, 116, 141, 195, 200, 201, 202, 203, 204, 221, 231, 243, 245, 252, 254, 256, 258, 259, 260, 262, 265, 279, 281, 282, 359, 363, 440, 469, 509, 520, 569, 627, 762, 763, 813, 814, 816, 840, 875

STRIPE 1, 3, 4, 5, 6, 16, 18, 24, 42, 43, 44, 45, 46, 47, 51, 95, 105, 106, 129, 148, 218, 233, 234, 235, 246, 280, 281, 282, 294, 316, 317, 318, 319, 326, 328, 329, 330, 331, 332, 333, 335, 336, 337, 338, 339, 340, 341, 342, 343, 344, 345, 347, 348, 349, 350, 351, 352, 353, 358, 360, 361, 362, 364, 368, 383, 386, 392, 393, 394, 415, 416, 417, 418, 419, 420, 421, 424, 430, 434, 435, 439, 481, 517, 518, 519, 520, 572, 706, 708, 709, 715, 718, 719, 721, 729, 730, 736, 751, 754, 759, 763, 765, 767, 771, 772, 773, 780, 784, 787, 798, 800, 803, 804, 805, 806, 808, 815, 816, 817, 824, 827, 830, 840, 853, 860, 863, 864, 877, 878, 888, 912, 916, 917, 920, 952, 965, 969, 985, 986, 988, 989, 992, 997, 998

SWASTIKA/GOOD LUCK SYMBOL 55, 57, 71, 72, 73, 85, 89, 98, 106, 122, 124, 243, 247, 299, 300, 303, 325, 446, 447, 455, 479

TARTAN 587, 588, 589, 590, 591, 592, 593, 594, 595

TEARDROP *see* **BOTEH**

TRIANGLE 1, 3, 6, 7, 12, 14, 15, 18, 19, 20, 22, 24, 39, 48, 107, 116, 141, 147, 153, 195, 200, 201, 202, 203, 204, 221, 231, 249, 272, 273, 279, 294, 314, 330, 334, 350, 355, 357, 359, 364, 365, 367, 369, 375, 376, 381, 387, 411, 415, 424, 426, 427, 437, 438, 448, 455, 479, 482, 494, 517, 518, 519, 526, 571, 657, 675, 721, 722, 733, 735, 738, 739, 743, 759, 764, 775, 778, 808, 840, 851, 854, 855, 866, 875, 898, 904, 961, 966, 970, 983, 986, 1000

WAVE 61, 88, 94, 103, 113, 114, 127, 140, 150, 249, 261, 289, 315, 321, 377, 405, 659, 663, 720, 771, 888; *see also* **SCROLL; SPIRAL; WATER**

X *see* **CROSS**

ZIGZAG 2, 3, 4, 11, 15, 21, 24, 106, 129, 148, 150, 182, 196, 198, 245, 246, 275, 277, 278, 279, 280, 285, 294, 340, 356, 360, 365, 367, 372, 375, 378, 379, 380, 381, 382, 383, 386, 388, 389, 390, 391, 392, 394, 395, 403, 407, 409, 415, 416, 417, 419, 420, 426, 430, 438, 544, 574, 709, 738, 752, 770, 799, 800, 810, 878, 879, 910, 986, 987, 988

ZIL-I-SOLTAN 193, 208, 500

NATURAL SHAPES

ANIMAL 48, 56, 130, 145, 153, 157, 163, 179, 205, 206, 209, 224, 246, 247, 256, 259, 275, 284, 308, 310, 344, 377, 387, 396, 398, 399, 400, 401, 402, 405, 410, 412, 413, 414, 421, 424, 426, 454, 485, 502, 503, 504, 516, 524, 530, 532, 543, 545, 549, 629, 640, 712, 769, 770, 811, 812, 830, 831, 832, 833, 834, 835, 841, 848, 873, 893, 926; *see also* **WINGED DOG/HORSE/LION**

BAMBOO 57, 86, 89, 90, 98, 108, 112, 135, 711

BIOLOGY *see* **SCIENCE**

BIRD 25, 26, 27, 29, 31, 35, 36, 38, 40, 50, 97, 102, 114, 118, 127, 143, 151, 157, 158, 163, 176, 187, 205, 208, 209, 212, 216, 217, 224, 289, 312, 344, 397, 410, 411, 412, 419, 421, 423, 425, 431, 468, 514, 521, 530, 543, 563, 566, 596, 597, 599, 610, 612, 614, 615, 623, 627, 631, 633, 638, 640, 657, 685, 740, 760, 770, 793, 809, 844, 873, 907, 950, 991; *see also* **MYTHICAL BIRD**

CLOUD 59, 71, 90, 98, 102, 111, 119, 140, 529, 727, 738, 811, 814, 912

FLOWER, GENERAL/UNIDENTIFIED 5, 23, 27, 28, 29, 30, 31, 32, 37, 38, 40, 41, 49, 53, 54, 56, 58, 60, 65, 66, 67, 68, 70, 72, 73, 77, 78, 79, 80, 81, 82, 83, 84, 85, 93, 97, 108, 115, 126, 132, 141, 144, 149, 151, 153, 158, 162, 163, 164, 165, 166, 170, 173, 174, 176, 177, 178, 179, 180, 181, 183, 184, 185, 186, 188, 190, 193, 194, 196, 197, 207, 208, 209, 213, 214, 215, 217, 219, 220, 222, 223, 225, 227, 228, 231, 232, 233, 238, 242, 248, 260, 264, 265, 266, 288, 290, 291, 301, 302, 304, 305, 309, 311, 312, 313, 323, 358, 412, 414, 436, 440, 444, 469, 471, 474, 478, 486, 487, 488, 489, 490, 491, 492, 493, 494, 495, 496, 497, 500, 501, 502, 506, 512, 515, 516, 526, 530, 531, 532, 533, 534, 539, 541, 542, 544, 545, 558, 565, 566, 567, 569, 574, 577, 578, 579, 580, 581, 584, 586, 596, 597, 598, 601, 602, 603, 606, 607, 610, 611, 616, 617, 618, 620, 621, 627, 628, 630, 632, 634, 635, 636, 637, 642, 643, 645, 646, 650, 651, 652, 653, 654, 655, 670, 671, 672, 674, 675, 679, 680, 684, 686, 691, 692, 700, 701, 704, 705, 706, 707, 711, 712, 713, 716, 724, 726, 732, 739, 740, 741, 743, 744, 745, 746, 748, 749, 753, 754, 758, 761, 782, 784, 788, 790, 793, 796, 800, 801, 809, 811, 823, 838, 859, 869, 870, 876, 885, 887, 889, 895, 905, 906, 909, 913, 918, 921, 922, 925, 930, 933, 934, 939, 945, 951, 953, 954, 961, 971, 977, 991; *see also* **ROSETTE**

FLOWER, SPECIFIC: ANEMONE 625, 631, 638; **CAMELLIA** 128; **CHERRY** 57, 104, 129, 133; **CHRYSANTHEMUM** 33, 47, 92, 102, 103, 109, 111, 125, 134, 137, 142, 622, 737, 755, 766, 777; **CLEMATIS** 191, 192; **CROCUS** 757; **DAFFODIL** 501, 669; **DAISY** 501, 624, 946, 960; **DANDELION** 658; **FUCHSIA** 211; **HOLLYHOCK** 122; **HONEYSUCKLE** 295, 306, 636; **HYACINTH** 241; **IRIS** 30, 110, 117, 127, 137, 605, 660, 661, 694, 695, 755, 984; **LILY** 47, 271, 482, 693; **LOTUS** 148, 160; **MARIGOLD** 647; **NARCISSUS** 756; **NASTURTIUM** 665, 696; **PAPYRUS** 287; **PAULOWNIA** 91, 111, 122; **PEACH**

BLOSSOM 94, 136, 142; **PEONY** 59, 63, 121, 123, 124, 137, 139, 755; **PLUM** 90, 98, 104, 132, 136, 138, 142; **POPPY** 641, 663, 685, 798, 928; **ROSE** 159, 210, 212, 240, 565, 614, 648, 715, 751, 785, 794, 810, 973, 986; **SUNFLOWER** 433, 441, 443, 445, 664; **THISTLE** 651; **TULIP** 143, 240, 241, 440, 441, 501, 609, 615, 648, 655, 681, 682, 697, 698, 707, 713, 734, 756, 807, 901, 986; **WATER LILY** 676, 678, 702, 703; **WISTERIA** 86, 135, 677

FRUIT, GENERAL 176, 521, 528, 543, 613, 626, 656, 662, 667, 683, 688, 689, 690, 699, 725, 770, 782, 792, 862, 891, 909

FRUIT, SPECIFIC: APPLE 608, 845, 878, 892, 962, 979; **BANANA** 87; **DATE** 291, 293; **FIG** 158; **GOURD** 653; **GRAPE/VINE** 34, 295, 305, 483, 484, 528, 529, 543, 644, 927; **PEACH** 795; **PEAR** 927; **PINEAPPLE** 225; **POMEGRANATE** 75, 76, 233, 237, 239, 241, 255, 271; **RASPBERRY** 489, 490; **STRAWBERRY** 596, 623

GRAIN 27, 816, 844

HUMAN FIGURE/PARTS OF THE BODY 21, 35, 69, 156, 157, 163, 181, 189, 205, 206, 209, 268, 269, 270, 282, 289, 292, 296, 344, 370, 380, 382, 385, 407, 412, 413, 422, 427, 428, 429, 431, 432, 440, 467, 514, 515, 521, 522, 523, 524, 525, 527, 528, 529, 530, 532, 534, 543, 548, 549, 550, 551, 557, 558, 559, 568, 619, 649, 722, 780, 812, 815, 830, 831, 832, 833, 834, 835, 841, 848, 868, 873, 893, 897, 900, 926; *see also* **COSTUME**

INSECT 26, 28, 29, 30, 32, 34, 54, 56, 59, 74, 121, 282, 411, 489, 490, 530, 531, 533, 534, 597, 666, 737, 790, 861, 886, 910, 956, 995

LEAF 1, 2, 8, 17, 21, 28, 29, 30, 31, 32, 33, 34, 35, 36, 37, 38, 53, 54, 57, 59, 63, 64, 65, 66, 67, 68, 69, 70, 73, 75, 76, 77, 78, 80, 81, 82, 83, 84, 86, 87, 89, 90, 91, 92, 93, 109, 110, 111, 112, 116, 117, 120, 121, 123, 124, 127, 128, 129, 133, 134, 137, 139, 142, 143, 148, 151, 157, 162, 164, 170, 172, 174, 175, 176, 177, 178, 180, 181, 183, 184, 185, 190, 191, 192, 193, 194, 196, 197, 209, 210, 211, 212, 213, 215, 219, 220, 222, 223, 232, 237, 240, 241, 248, 256, 259, 264, 265, 266, 288, 291, 295, 297, 301, 302, 304, 306, 307, 308, 309, 310, 311, 312, 313, 314, 315, 316, 317, 318, 319, 324, 412, 436, 440, 442, 444, 459, 465, 466, 469, 470, 471, 472, 473, 474, 475, 476, 477, 478, 483, 484, 485, 486, 488, 489, 490, 491, 492, 493, 495, 496, 497, 498, 500, 501, 502, 503, 504, 510, 511, 512, 513, 514, 515, 521, 522, 523, 524, 525, 528, 529, 530, 531, 532, 533, 534, 539, 541, 543, 544, 545, 546, 547, 548, 549, 552, 553, 555, 556, 558, 559, 561, 562, 563, 564, 578, 579, 580, 581, 582, 583, 585, 596, 597, 598, 599, 600, 601, 603, 606, 607, 608, 609, 610, 611, 613, 614, 615, 616, 617, 618, 620, 621, 622, 623, 624, 625, 626, 627, 628, 629, 630, 631, 632, 634, 635, 636, 637, 638, 639, 640, 641, 642, 643, 644, 645, 646, 647, 648, 649, 650, 651, 652, 653, 654, 655, 656, 657, 660, 661, 662, 663, 664, 665, 666, 667, 669, 670, 671, 672, 674, 675, 677, 678, 679, 680,

NATURAL SHAPES (continued)

MYTHOLOGICAL, RELIGIOUS, AND SYMBOLIC

ARTIFACTS

ARCHITECTURE 69, 157, 288, 313, 413, 515, 517, 518, 519, 527, 528, 567, 568, 575, 576, 738, 780, 812, 815, 819, 827, 829, 830, 831, 835, 843, 844, 857, 873, 874, 897, 943, 969, 985

COSTUME 35, 69, 138, 156, 157, 163, 180, 181, 292, 296, 385, 407, 427, 428, 429, 467, 521, 524, 525, 527, 528, 529, 534, 543, 550, 558, 568, 780, 812, 828, 830, 831, 832, 833, 834, 835, 837, 841, 873, 900; *see also* **HUMAN FIGURE**

ELECTRICAL 827, 839

HERALDIC DEVICE 40, 108, 122, 126

HOUSEHOLD ITEM 132, 157, 193, 208, 296, 500, 515, 521, 522, 529, 725, 866, 869, 891, 981

TOOL/WEAPON/INSTRUMENT 9, 10, 35, 156, 428, 429, 522, 524, 525, 528, 558, 560, 563, 564, 619, 649, 812, 816, 818, 832, 841, 854, 857, 886,

TRANSPORTATION 25, 40, 287, 568, 811, 814, 825, 829, 831, 849, 957, 961

NAMED PERIODS/ART MOVEMENTS

ART NOUVEAU 649, 650, 651, 652, 653, 654, 655, 656, 657, 658, 659, 660, 661, 662, 663, 664, 665, 666, 667, 668, 669, 670, 671, 672, 673, 674, 675, 676, 677, 678, 679, 680, 681, 682, 683, 684, 685, 686, 687, 688, 689, 690, 691, 692, 693, 694, 695, 696, 697, 698, 699, 700, 701, 702, 703, 704, 895, 984

ARTS & CRAFTS 596, 597, 598, 599, 600, 601, 602, 603, 604, 605, 606, 607, 608, 609, 610, 611, 612, 613, 614, 615, 616, 617, 618, 619, 620, 621, 622, 623, 624, 625, 626, 627, 628, 629, 630, 631, 632, 633, 634, 635, 636, 637, 638, 639, 640, 641, 642, 643, 644, 645, 646, 647, 648

BAROQUE & ROCOCO 543, 544, 545, 546, 547, 548, 549, 550, 551, 552, 553, 554, 555, 556, 557, 558, 559, 560, 561, 562, 563, 564

EARLY 20TH-CENTURY 31, 32, 33, 37, 45, 46, 121, 129, 158, 160, 240, 241, 243, 244, 246, 247, 248, 289, 292, 326, 331, 332, 333, 334, 338, 341, 361, 364, 437, 438, 439, 573, 705, 706, 707, 708, 709, 710, 711, 712, 713, 714, 715, 716, 717, 718, 719, 720, 721, 722, 723, 724, 725, 726, 727, 728, 729, 730, 731, 732, 733, 734, 735, 736, 737, 738, 739, 740, 741, 742, 743, 744, 745, 746, 747, 748, 749, 750, 751, 752, 753, 754, 755, 756, 757, 758, 759, 760, 761, 762, 763, 764, 765, 766, 767, 768, 769, 770, 771, 772, 773, 774, 775, 776, 777, 778, 779, 780, 781, 782, 783, 784, 785, 786, 787, 788, 789, 790, 791, 792, 793, 794, 795, 796, 797, 798, 799, 800, 801, 802, 803, 804, 805, 806, 807, 808, 809, 810, 811, 812, 813, 814, 815, 816

MEDIEVAL 465, 466, 467, 468, 469, 470, 471, 472, 473, 474, 475, 476, 477, 478, 479, 480, 481, 482, 483, 484, 485, 486, 487, 488, 489, 490, 491, 492, 493, 494, 495, 496, 497, 498, 499, 500, 843, 908

1980s TO THE PRESENT 30, 42, 43, 93, 99, 100, 128, 139, 140, 179, 354, 355, 381, 384, 385, 410, 411, 414, 415, 418, 421, 422, 423, 424, 985, 986, 987, 988, 989, 990, 991, 992, 993, 994, 995, 996, 997, 998, 999, 1000

1940s & 1950s 21, 22, 23, 28, 29, 33, 50, 53, 90, 98, 125, 156, 329, 349, 357, 359, 382, 416, 417, 817, 818, 819, 820, 821, 822, 823, 824, 825, 826, 827, 828, 829, 830, 831, 832, 833, 834, 835, 836, 837, 838, 839, 840, 841, 842, 843, 844, 845, 846, 847, 848, 849, 850, 851, 852, 853, 854, 855, 856, 857, 859, 860, 861, 862, 863, 864, 865, 866, 867, 868, 869, 870, 871, 872, 873, 874, 875, 876, 877, 878, 879, 880, 881, 882, 883, 884, 885, 886, 887, 990

1960s & 1970s 18, 19, 20, 21, 22, 23, 383, 413, 888, 889, 890, 891, 892, 893, 894, 895, 896, 897, 898, 899, 900, 901, 902, 903, 904, 905, 906, 907, 908, 909, 910, 911, 912, 913, 914, 915, 916, 917, 918, 919, 920, 921, 922, 923, 924, 925, 926, 927, 928, 929, 930, 931, 932, 933, 934, 935, 936, 937, 938, 939, 940, 941, 942, 943, 944, 945, 946, 947, 948, 949, 950, 951, 952, 953, 954, 955, 956, 957, 958, 959, 960, 961, 962, 963, 964, 965, 966, 967, 968, 969, 970, 971, 972, 973, 974, 975, 976, 977, 978, 979, 980, 981, 982, 983, 984

19TH-CENTURY 5, 6, 7, 41, 47, 48, 49, 59, 61, 63, 64, 65, 66, 67, 68, 69, 70, 71, 72, 74, 75–80, 91, 92, 94, 95, 96, 97, 101, 102, 103, 105, 106, 107, 108, 110, 111, 112, 113, 114, 115, 118, 119, 120, 123, 124, 126, 127, 130, 132, 134, 135, 136, 138, 141, 142, 154, 157, 159, 163, 164, 169, 170, 171, 172, 173, 175, 180, 181, 196, 209, 210, 211, 215, 217, 221, 223, 234, 235, 236, 238, 240, 256, 257, 260, 261, 262, 283, 287, 288, 290, 291, 293, 308, 320, 321, 322, 323, 334, 335, 336, 340, 358, 362, 363, 386, 387, 388, 389, 393, 395, 396, 397, 398, 399, 400, 401, 402, 405, 410, 420, 433, 434, 435, 436, 440, 441, 442, 444, 445, 497, 498, 499, 500, 517, 518, 519, 565, 566, 567, 568, 569, 570, 571, 572, 573, 574, 575, 576, 577, 578, 579, 580, 581, 582, 583, 584, 585, 586, 587, 588, 589, 590, 591, 592, 593, 594, 595

RENAISSANCE 501, 502, 503, 504, 505, 506, 507, 508, 509, 510, 511, 512, 513, 514, 515, 516, 517, 518, 519, 520, 521, 522, 523, 524, 525, 526, 527, 528, 529, 530, 531, 532, 533, 534, 535, 536, 537, 538, 539, 540, 541, 542

Introduction

This book is a compilation of patterns from around the world. They have been sourced from archive collections of ceramics, textiles, and other decorative surfaces held in museums and by private collectors. Some patterns have been included because they are the highest representation of that area's art available; some are included purely because of their decorative appeal. All are the result of an artist or artisan's desire to produce something of beauty.

Each section of the book runs geographically and includes, where possible, examples from the time before chemical, synthetic dyes were widespread. Efforts have also been made to include patterns that have been produced by hand, by means of painting, embroidery, or weaving.

The majority of the patterns shown are textile designs—either actual examples of the printed or embroidered cloth or the original hand-rendered designs. This is not an unfair bias, and other areas and media are not neglected, but a culture's textiles, more readily portable and affordable than many other media, usually offer us its broadest range of pattern and the fullest realization of its design skills.

What is pattern?

Pattern is ubiquitous—we wear it, cover our walls and floors with it, sit on it, eat off it, and even sleep on it! Patterns surround us continually as we observe the objects in our world and we begin to see regularity in them. We see pattern in pebbles on a beach, leaves lying on the grass, and stars gleaming in the sky. At every moment and on every side, patterns of varying size, color, and definition encircle us. Pattern can be purely ornamental—a pleasing decoration—or it can have enormous religious and cultural significance, saving us from demons and promoting good fortune. Throughout history patterns have used symbolic motifs, specific colors, and well-established designs to give meaning and continuity to the messages they contained. Even today, many Eastern countries, in particular, use a restricted color palette and ancient symbols in their decoration of major buildings. In China, for example, the colors red, green (or gold), white, and black dominate their architecture and art. To the Chinese these colors represent more than just their visual richness: each one may also be a compass direction, a season, a quality, an animal, and even an emotion.

The dictionary definition of pattern is an ornamental design; we know it best as the recurrence of similar forms at regular intervals. Each ornamental form can be termed a "motif" and the way in which they regularly occur is called "the repeat."

The main lines on which repeats are constructed are few, simple, and well established. The art of the surface pattern designer is to arrange them in such a way as to make a pleasing balanced composition in terms of color, layout, and scale—whether for textiles, ceramics, or any other decorative surface and to make the resulting design "fit for purpose."

A good pattern always has an underlying symmetry. This is necessary for the look and structure of the pattern in its own right and also to fit in with manufacturing requirements—such as the width of a loom or the size of a tile.

Structure

The simplest of all patterns is the stripe, which is a series of parallel lines that run either horizontally or vertically. Sometimes these are altered to give us the zigzag.

Stripes give a strong directional emphasis whenever they are worn or placed on an interior or exterior surface room. For example, we are all familiar with the idea that vertical stripes make the wearer taller, or a room seem higher, while horizontal ones make an object seem wider, or a ceiling lower. Stripes in both directions give the lattice or grid, which forms the underlying structure for a large number of patterns, such as the tapa designs from Polynesia, which are almost all based upon a basic grid, loosely squared up.

If the angle at which the two lines cross is altered we get the diamond, which is a potent design shape in its own right. However, by introducing a third line and bisecting the diamond laterally, we get an equilateral triangle, which is the basis for an infinity of patterns, using not only the triangle and diamond but also the hexagon, which is six triangles arranged together.

A fourth series of lines gives the octagon, which forms the basis of yet more radiating patterns. These shapes compounded give the complex, intricate, and ingenious variety of patterns we see on tiled, pierced, and painted mosque and palace floor, wall, and window treatments prevalent throughout the Islamic world because they conform to the Islamic instruction of being geometric in origin.

Many of the above patterns can also be drawn using curved lines and by incorporating circles or arcs. However, the underlying structure is always the square, rectangle, diamond, or triangle already described.

It can be observed that certain kinds of ornament are in harmony with a particular type of construction line. For instance, naturalistic forms complement curving free-flowing lines, and formal patterns suit rigid geometric lines. Certain types of design style have centered upon a type of line—for example, patterns of the Art Nouveau movement were based upon a curving sinuous line, while Bauhaus designs are necessarily based upon a rectilinear line.

The characteristic lines of well-established patterns are generally the direct result of the restrictions that the designer has had to abide by. In other words, although certain styles of design may be associated with a particular design period or place, it is almost always the case that a technical or practical reason had to be satisfied. This is generally to do with the methods of production. For instance, the Wiener Werkstätte designs were all block-printed by hand and have the crispness and clarity associated with that method; early engraved roller-printed textiles continued the practice of copperplate printers, who often used images derived from engravings; ceramic patterns have to fit the size of the tile or the shape of object onto which they are to be painted or printed, and so on. As with most endeavors, the practicalities must always be addressed first.

All these patterns, whether for ceramics, textiles, or other decorative surfaces, are the result of considerable planning and expertise. However, quite often, once a reliable formula has been worked out, it is used over and over again, in endless variations, only changing in color, texture, and dimensions.

Thus, once the pattern has been sketched out, the designer may alter the look of it by means of various devices that make considered use of scale, contrast, and texture. An example would be the counterchange, whereby adjacent parts are alternately colored light and dark. Another device is the turnover, which takes a motif or part of a design and flips it horizontally or vertically. This can form a mirror-repeat or not, depending on the placement. The turnover is a particularly important element in woven textile design and ceramic tiles. The superimposition of one pattern onto another subtler pattern is another well-established device, often used by William Morris in his many surface pattern designs.

Repeat

For a pattern to be produced by mechanical means, it has to appear to join seamlessly across the width and length of the fabric, paper, or wall onto which it is to appear. The process of doing this is termed "putting the design into repeat" and can often be a highly skilled operation. The finished design must flow well in all directions and should avoid the mechanical effect of too-obvious repetition. Also, it should not show any obvious breaks or distracting areas of pattern, light, or shade, as unplanned irregularities may spoil the look of the whole design.

Once the parameters of scale have been decided, the central features of the design can be placed in such a way that they occur next to themselves in a "side-by-side" repeat. Alternatively, the motifs can be slightly dropped down next to the original placing to give a "drop" repeat. This can be at half the original length of the main design to give a "half-drop" repeat, or at lesser or greater intervals, dependent on the desired result. The repeat can also be staggered horizontally, giving a "brick repeat," most often used in architecture and ceramics.

Patterns that are based on diamonds or the equivalent rounded "ogee" shapes are known as "false drops," because they are worked out on square lines and are not dropped at all. A great many late Gothic weaves are designed on this principle.

Another method of repeat is that perfected by weavers in their invention of the sateen weaves, which give rise to "spot repeats." This is a system whereby the danger of apparent lines in small repeats is minimized by the careful placing of the motifs in relation to one another. The resulting pattern is often called a "diaper" pattern and is frequently used in textile designs.

The direction of the repeat is determined by its end use. For instance, wallpaper designs are almost always one-way designs, as are wall tiles. Floor tiles and the majority of apparel (clothing) designs are "allover" designs, as this serves the manufacturer by not creating wastage. The scale of the design is also dependent on its end use; for example, furnishing designs are generally large, as befits the size of the drapes or large items of furniture that they will cover, while dress designs are usually small or medium in scale, again depending on the area of fabric that will be used and the desired effect. Many designs may be enlarged for one end use or reduced for another.

Textile designs are frequently categorized by the type of ornament that they employ. This traditionally gives us four categories—

floral; geometric or abstract; conversational (usually artifacts; literally any object one could have a conversation about); and ethnic. Fashions for and within each category change subtly, giving us, for example, the strong naturalistic and abstracted shapes of the 1950s and 1960s, which mellowed into the quirky and bold abstract designs of the 1970s. Floral designs are the most consistently popular patterns of all.

The use of color is of paramount importance in pattern design. Today there is an enormous range of colors available, thanks to the inventions of chemists over the last two centuries. Before the 1800s, designers had only natural dyestuffs to work with, which were liable to fade and wash out and required great skill to use them properly. We have the great Victorian craftsman William Morris to thank for researching and documenting the old methods of dyeing using madder, indigo, weld, and other natural dyes. The continued popularity of his designs today means that we can still see examples of these natural dye colors, even if many of his works are now reproduced by chemical means.

The immense range of patterns in this book, drawn from a wide variety of sources and styles, nonetheless all share a geometric underlying structure and the positive aim of delighting the eye of the beholder.

Enjoy!

The patterns in this section are taken from a wide variety of cultures, covering a time when artifacts were produced individually and decorated by hand. Largely produced out of our need to surround ourselves with items of beauty, these patterns take their inspiration from the natural world or the geometric order we impose onto it. They are often also used as symbols to ward off impending disaster, and many cultures used specific motifs and colors for this purpose—

the vane-swastika or good-luck symbol is a good example of this practice. Undoubtedly, the majority of early patterns were commissioned with this purpose in mind, and the skill, time, and money invested in their production reflected the status of the tribe or clan that produced them. Ordinary working people also wished for beautiful, auspicious, or religiously significant

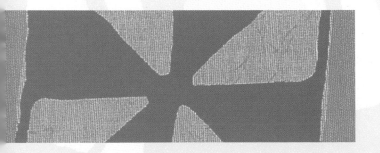

Part One
Pre-Industrial

decorations and this is reflected in many of the exquisitely worked embroideries, weaves, prints, and painted patterns in this section. In it we find such diverse examples as the convoluted patterns of medieval monks, incredibly detailed designs from the Orient and Near East, patchworks of the early settlers to the United States, and the many woven fabrics that represent hours of labor, collecting, spinning, and dyeing the yarn, and creating the intricacies of the design. The colors used are often the result of the subtle muted shades of natural dyestuffs; more recent examples use chemical dyes to produce their bright hues. All these patterns are an expression of people's instinctive love of decoration.

Oceania
Polynesia

1 *Variety is the hallmark of this richly patterned tapa, or siapo, barkcloth from Niue, an island between Tonga and the Cook Islands. The cloth is made from the inner bark of the paper mulberry tree. To create the pattern, the cloth was divided into a primary grid and then subdivided, and the various frames within the subdivisions were then blocked in with freehand designs.*

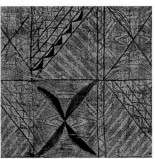

2–4 *The zigzag chip-carved designs typically found on Samoan spears and clubs were no doubt an inspiration for these three original Pacific Island patterns. The abstract shapes and plant forms in each pattern have been drawn with a mixture of fine and broad lines, resulting in a satisfying counterbalance between color and space. An examination of part-finished barkcloths suggests that designs such as these were meticulously worked out to fill the planned grid layout.*

Many of the motifs prevalent throughout the world are said to stem from the Pacific region, especially the eight- or twelve-pointed star shape and the so-called wind vane or vane swastika or good luck motif. The islands of Polynesia have traditionally used a type of cloth called tapa or barkcloth, which is derived from the inner bark of certain trees. To produce their designs, they are first carved in wood and then transferred to the barkcloth by rubbing over them with dye. They are frequently overpainted by means of a makeshift paintbrush. Often several people at once will have a hand in decorating the tapas. These traditional cloths are used for apparel, ceremonial wear, and as general household textiles. They remain some of the few textiles still being made and decorated entirely by hand.

Oceania
Polynesia 2

5 *Fish are depicted in astonishing detail on this large barkcloth or* ngatu *from Tonga, which dates from the 19th century. To produce the design, the part-dyed cloth was first folded and rubbed with pigment in order to create the guide grid, and then stenciled with the fish motif. Finally, it was overpainted to give emphasis to selected parts of the pattern.*

6–7 *These two geometric designs, both from the 19th century, are characteristic Fijian cloths that have been decorated by means of a stencil cut from a banana leaf. The technique involves first marking out a grid and then rubbing the stencils with dye, working across the cloth from side to center until the pattern is complete.*

8 *A design resembling leaves or pods has been painted freehand onto this barkcloth, or tapa, from Vanuatu. It recalls the patterns found on the island's famous openwork braided mats. Patterned barkcloth is, however, comparatively rare in Vanuatu.*

9–10 *Pattern design is not a static phenomenon but constantly evolves to reflect new developments and events. Compare these two Fijian cloths: the earlier design, (9), shows spearlike symbols pointing toward a central star. A later cloth, (10), features a stencil-printed muzzle-loading musket motif, complete with trigger guard, ramrod, percussion hammer, and surrounding gunshot starbursts.*

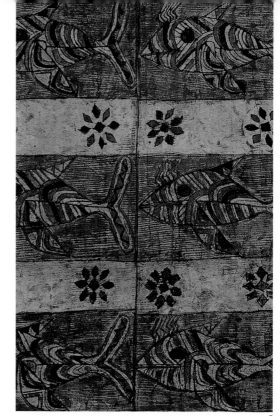

5

6

7

9

8

10

Oceania
Polynesia 3

11 *A dominant large zigzag motif is echoed by small zigzag infills in this modern version of a typical Polynesian pattern. Factory-made, it lacks the delightful idiosyncrasies found in hand-printed textiles, but it remains a striking design.*

12 *Much of the appeal of traditional Polynesian pattern springs from the fact that the village women who printed the designs were able to improvise freely within a basic grid. In this barkcloth, most of the grid squares are blocked out with nine triangles, but the edge contains a line of larger grid squares blocked out with 12 triangles. This out-of-step sequencing makes the pattern vibrant and exciting.*

13 *Stencils cut from banana leaves were used to produce the "papercut"-style motifs seen in this pattern. Each leaf stencil was placed within a grid, and the colored pigment then rubbed over it. Once the basic forms of these motifs were in place, the frames were blocked in with color to give them greater emphasis.*

14 *The almost three-dimensional effect of this amazingly intricate pattern is due to the way it was produced. First, the cloth was folded, creased, and rubbed with pigment so that the guide grid was clearly marked out. Then, each square within the grid was printed by means of a rubbed wooden block; and finally, the whole work was painstakingly overpainted by hand.*

15 *The serrated pattern that makes up this 20th-century design takes its inspiration from chip carving. This traditional woodworking technique involves using small knives to pattern wood with rows of triangular nicks or chips.*

16 *Parallel lines with a triangular infill make up this modern woven pattern. The design recalls those seen on ceremonial chip-carved paddle blades and on traditional rub-printed barkcloths.*

17 *Red, brown, and off-white shapes play against each other to form a dynamic, kaleidoscope-like pattern. This liveliness is the result of using two rubbing blocks to print the design. Once a guide grid had been created, the cloth was held taut over a chip-carved and incised wooden block and rubbed with colored dye. This process was then repeated with the second block. The holes in the block show on the cloth as the unprinted part of the pattern.*

11

12

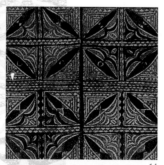
14

13

15

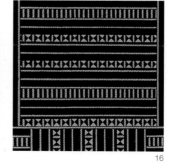
16

Oceania
Polynesia 4

18–20 *Bold and colorful, these patterns straddle two very different cultures. During the 1960s, many Western designers became fascinated by so-called "primitive" crafts and began to look to ethnic and tribal sources for inspiration. In many cases they simply collected random batches of ethnic fabrics and lifted the designs directly from the pattern. The two 1960s patterns on the left (18 and 19) and the pattern in the center (20) are clearly motifs that have been taken from a Polynesian source,* almost certainly a barkcloth. They have, however, been somewhat "tidied up" in order to suit Western silk-screen printing techniques. The large pattern at center (**20**) is particularly interesting: with its clean lines and jumping color counterchange it is a typical example of a 1960s printed fabric, but there is no denying that at its heart it is a Polynesian pattern.

18

19

21–23 The three patterns on the right—all characteristic examples of printed patterns that were produced in the West in the 1950s and 1960s—draw their inspiration from traditional Polynesian barkcloths. This is borne out by the use of the figure-eight motif, the heavily stylized flowers, the zigzag pattern infill, and the color-block counterchange set within a grid. As to why Western designers were so happy to copy the designs, the answer has to do with the way the original Polynesian cloths were printed. When Western designers saw how the patterns had been produced by stretching barkcloth over carved blocks and then rubbing colors through—a printing technique that resulted in a design of one or more colors on a white ground—they immediately realized that, with a minimum of design effort, they could produce much the same patterns using modern silk-screen presses.

21

20

22

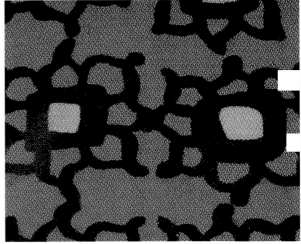

23

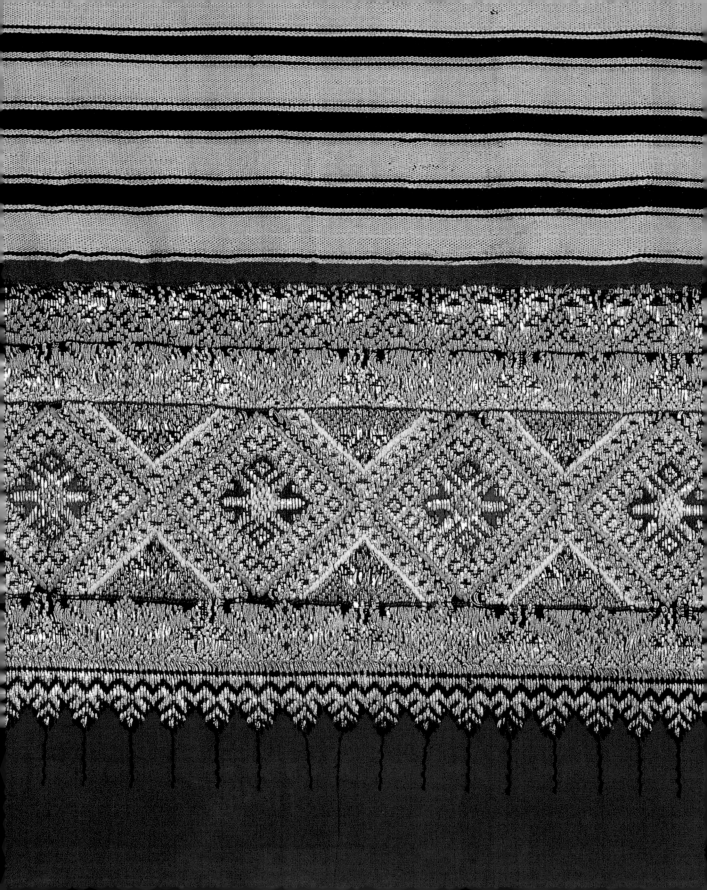

Southeast Asia
Indonesia

24

25

26

27

24 *Made in Sumatra, this sumptuous woven silk sari has been created by first setting up the loom for a plain weave and then by hand-brocading gilt weft threads into the plain warp. The richness of the pattern suggests that it was made for a special ceremonial occasion.*

25 *A charming sarong made using the batik technique. This involves repeatedly wax-printing a resist design on a plain woven cloth, dipping the cloth in dye so that the waxed areas resist the color, and then ironing to remove the wax.*

26 *This Javanese sarong depicts a collection of animals that were thought to have mystical powers. The boldness of the design suggests that it is a man's sarong.*

27 *The imagery of birds and flowers on this sarong—swallows and ears of corn or rice—and the way that the images are placed tells us that it was designed to be worn by a mature married woman.*

The majority of the printed patterns in this section derive from Java, which has a long and rich tradition of decorating cloths for apparel, ritual, or domestic purposes. Cloths are woven from cotton or silk and decorated using a carefully drawn or blocked pattern of molten beeswax that resists the dyes. The vibrant colors shown here are often chemical dyes, but all cloths produced before the beginning of the 19th century would have used vegetable or mineral dyes. The choice of color is related to the age and perceived status of the recipient with pastel colors being used for the young, full reds and blues for the mature woman, and grays, purples, and darker colors for older patrons. The batiks use motifs that have symbolic meanings or are stylized naturalistic forms, sometimes drawn in the European style for the Western market.

Southeast Asia
Indonesia 2

28 *A beautiful batik floral sarong made in the Peranakan style in Java, by Oey Soe Tjoen Kedoengwoeni, sometime about 1950. The pattern was created by hand-drawing a wax resist onto a plain machine-woven cotton cloth. The color counterchange design, with its characteristic butterfly-and-bouquet motif, is a special feature of the artist's work.*

29 *Signed "Pekalonga," this fine batik sarong bears the stamped mark of Geo. Wehry & Co. This tells us that it was made in Java for a Dutch trading firm sometime in the 1950s. The sarong was designed to be worn by a mature married woman: the motif of small chicks is a characteristic "code," designed to tell the world that the wearer was a prosperous lady with plenty of grandchildren.*

30 *The batik artist Oey Soe Tjoen Kedoengwoeni drew inspiration from Chinese designs for this cotton cloth, made in Java in the 1980s. The arrangement of the patterns and motifs suggests that the cloth was designed not to be worn as a sarong but rather to be hung on the wall like a tapestry.*

31 *This high-cost, top-quality batik cotton sarong was made in Java by Lies van Zuylen, an Indo-European artist, sometime between 1900 and 1910. The way the hand-drawn wax resist was painstakingly spaced so that it filled the available ground made it expensive to produce. The high price and the use of late summer flowers within the motifs tells us that this cloth was designed to be worn by a prosperous middle-aged Indo-European woman.*

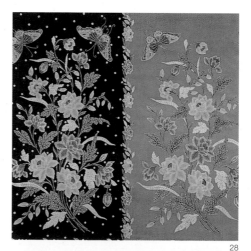

28

29

32 *Designed and produced for the local market, this batik sarong was made in Java in 1937 by Lies van Zuylen. The motifs on cloths of this type and character had little or no significance, other than to suggest that the wearer was delicate and refined.*

33 *During World War II, square batik appliqués such as this were produced in Indonesia for officers of the occupying Japanese army. This example was made in Java in 1943. It is likely that the army officers specially requested the use of the chrysanthemum motif, a Japanese symbol of long life and happiness. The glazed silklike finish was achieved by burnishing the cloth with a wine bottle.*

30

31

32

33

Southeast Asia
Indonesia

34 *A 20th-century fabric that draws its inspiration from Indonesian ethnic tradition. While it uses characteristic motifs—butterflies and vines with the dotted infill—the spacing and the overall regularity of the motifs tells us that this is machine-printed.*

35 *The designer of this machine-printed fabric has chosen a seemingly traditional Indonesian motif. Shadow puppets, however, have little connection with traditional Indonesian textiles.*

36 *This detail comes from a beautifully handworked Javanese batik sarong. The overall design reflects the batik workers' view of their universe: in the upper world (seen here) there are birds and flying creatures, and in the lower world fish and serpents.*

37 *This sarong, made in the first decade of the 20th century, dates to a time when pressure for increased production from*

Chinese and European traders began to affect the shape of the patterns and motifs. Village women who once made the batiks for pleasure now did the process in a rush, with the effect that the images are less defined.

38 *This Javanese sarong is a wonderful example of canting work. Wax is broken into small pieces and put into a long-spouted brass canting—rather like a miniature kettle. The canting is heated and the liquid wax is trailed over the cloth to mark out the lines of the design. The cloth is then dipped into the dye, and finally ironed to remove the wax.*

39 *A mix of block printing and wax trailing was used to make this modern batik cloth. The ground was divided into a square grid and then subdivided to create triangles within squares within squares. The small squares were worked with a block dipped in wax, and finally the whole design overworked with trailed wax.*

40 *This wax-trailed Javanese batik sarong was most likely intended as a wedding gift. This is borne out by the inclusion of motifs relating to clan prosperity: cockerels for male virility, ships for abundance, and a heraldic motif or coat of arms for the groom's family.*

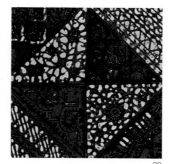

39

Southeast Asia
Indonesia 4

41 *A woven cloth made in Western Indonesia in the last quarter of the 19th century. While the strong flowerlike motifs point to this being a woven ikat cloth, the crispness of the outlines belies the fact and suggests that this cloth was possibly created by a technique of adding weft strands to an otherwise plain warp.*

42 *Offered as a funeral gift, this woven sapang or shoulder cloth dates from the 1980s. It was made in the town of Ngada in Flores, a region famous for its supplementary weft cloths. This technique involves painstakingly adding brightly colored weft threads to an otherwise plain cloth.*

43 *On a blue-black ground, a variety of geometrical motifs float between lines of brightly colored weft. Sarongs of this type are one-sided: on the plain side, the weft motifs only show as small dashes or picks of weft thread floating over the warp. This woven sarong was made in the Manggarai region of Flores in the early 1980s.*

44 *While this sarong was made in Sumatra using ikat techniques— meaning the warp threads were tied and dyed before being woven—the strength of the colors and their unusual arrangement suggest that the weaver drew inspiration from outside influences, perhaps from the Philippines.*

41

42

45 *Ikat cloths are characterized by the motifs being blurred in the direction of the warp—or you might say there appears to be a color bleed that runs parallel to the length of the cloth. This woven ikat cloth was made in the Sikka region of Flores in the early 20th century.*

46 *A hand-trailed, wax-resist Javanese sarong made in the first quarter of the 20th century. This characteristic design is known as* parang rusak, *meaning a broken daggerlike rock. Legend has it that it was created by the Sultan Agung, the first Muslim ruler. The story tells how he drew inspiration from the jagged rocky coasts of the region.*

47 *Autumn-flowering chrysanthemums are framed by an outer border of lilies on this Javanese sarong. The subtle, rather quiet, colors of this piece tell us that it was designed for an older woman. The cloth was made by Lien Metzelar in the last years of the 19th century.*

44

45

46

47

43

Southeast Asia
Indonesia 5

48 *The triangular forms used on this late 19th-century Javanese batik sarong reflect the traditional northern Javanese style of much older block-printed forms. In this example, the classic form has been mixed with modern animal motifs to create a high-quality prestigious cloth.*

49 *The traditional "Sawat" (large wings) motif found on this Javanese batik waistcoat (probably dating to the 19th century) represents the Tree of Life and the garuda—a birdlike creature from Hindu-Javanese mythology that carried Vishnu through the heavens.*

50 *The vertical direction of the blur within the stylized birds and Tree of Life motif on this 1940s ikat indicates a warp ikat—meaning the warp threads were organized, and then tied and dyed, all before they were mounted on the loom.*

51 *While the cloth from this sarong is Indonesian, the motifs, dragons, snakes, and shrimps, all derive from Chinese traditions. The weaver has used two techniques, a floating weft for the white dragons and a tied-and-dyed ikat weft for the motifs on the red ground.*

52 *The large motifs in this example are the stylized wings of the garuda—a mythical*

bird—while the "sprouting" or "growing" motifs represent fertility. This particular design is one of the "forbidden" patterns, from a time in the 18th century when the sultans decreed that certain patterns were banned to commoners.

53 *Traditionally there were patterned cloths for each and every occasion—weddings, births, and funerals for example. In the 1940s, however, when there was a shortage of cloth, the printers developed multipatterned cloth featuring stylized flowers and foliage, which could be worn for just about every occasion.*

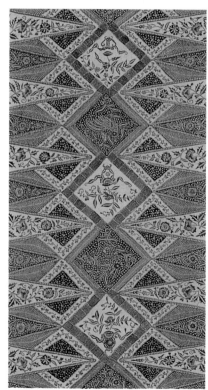

48

49

51

50

52

54

55

56

57

East Asia
China

54 *The flowing patterns on this vase were created using a technique similar to cloisonné work. Heavy-bodied glaze is trailed over the part-fired pot so that the primary lines of the design stand up in slight relief.*

55 *Tessellating patterns of this type are found all over the Far East. The never-ending pattern is made up of a single motif—color counterchanged and mirror reversed—that has a swastika or good luck symbol at its heart.*

56 *On this woven silk fabric the stylized bats symbolize longevity and the butterflies happiness. The everlasting knot—a motif that seems to cross time, space, and cultures—symbolizes eternity.*

57 *A woven and embroidered fabric comprising naturalistic bamboo stems to signify youth and long life, and cherry blossoms for beauty. Interspersed is a stylized chi symbol for good luck; note the miniature swastikas within the chi symbol.*

China has a long and honorable tradition of exquisite pattern-making in all the decorative arts, including textiles, ceramics, and painting. Many of the motifs used have a special relevance to the diverse Chinese cultures and religions or derive from ancient Chinese mythology. Favorable emblems such as cranes, phoenixes, peonies, and plum blossoms are regularly used to ensure good luck, prosperity, happiness, and longevity. For maximum effect, they are often depicted with Chinese characters, such as chi, signifying life and energy. One of the most potent symbols in Chinese pattern-making is the dragon. This fearsome beast is found in many guises, but always exemplifies male power and yang energy. The constant appurtenance of the dragon is a ball, variously interpreted as the sun, the moon, or the pearl of potentiality.

East Asia
China 2

58

59

58 *A silk-and-gilt-thread, tapestry-woven mirror case made in the mid-17th century. At the center of the design is a characteristic mythical bird: the phoenix or feng. The phoenix is a female symbol that promises a bounteous harvest and a prosperous ripeness—a perfect wedding gift.*

59 *Symbolic motifs abound in this 19th-century fabric. The dragon represents male strength and vitality, peonies and clouds symbolize a harmonious future, and butterflies stand for marital bliss and fidelity.*

The gold background indicates that the fabric was intended for the emperor or one of his descendants.

60 *Made sometime in the middle of the 18th century, this exquisitely embroidered silk hanging is said to have hung in the Imperial Palace. This story is borne out by the embroidery's subject matter—the five dragons with the pearl at the center—and the fact that the motifs are worked on a gold ground. Yellow or gold was known as the color of control and was reserved for the emperor and his descendants.*

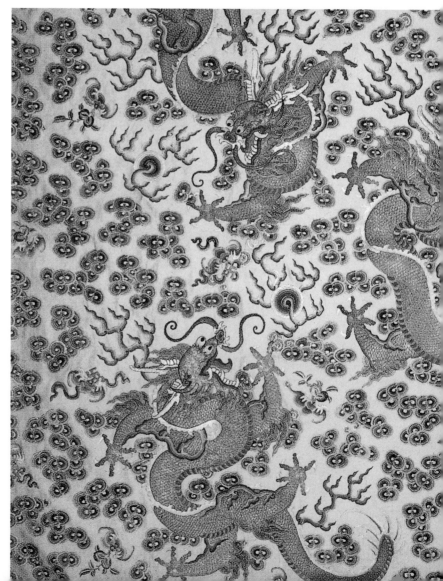

61 *"Slit tapestry" is the weaving technique used to create this silk fabric. If you look at the pattern closely you will see how, with the warp running along the length of the cloth, the pattern was achieved by running weft threads across the width of the warp. The slits mark the point in the block of color where an individual weft thread loops around a warp thread to make its return journey. This fragment comes from a garment, possibly a cuff or band, made in the mid-19th century at the time of the Ching dynasty.*

62 *The use of the chi-lin (Chinese unicorn) motif set on a gold ground tells us that this garment was part of the ceremonial regalia. It was probably worn by a high-ranking official, possibly an imperial son-in-law. This embroidered silk-and-gilt-thread cloth was made sometime at the beginning of the 17th century.*

61

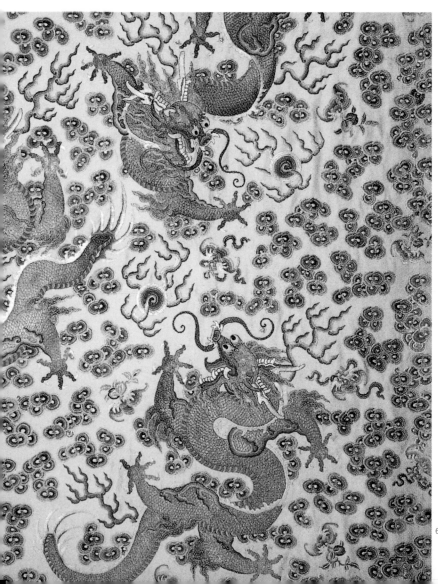

62

60

East Asia
China 3

63

64

63 *"Chinoiserie"—the taste
for decoration based on Chinese
design—was immensely popular
in Europe during the 19th century.
This late 19th-century wallpaper,
featuring stylized peonies, draws
its inspiration from an early
19th-century Chinese vase.*

64 *A mid-19th-century European
interpretation of an earlier 19th-
century Chinese design. When
European designers saw patterns
and motifs of this character, they
stripped them from their original
context and used them in every
kind of application, from wallpapers
and fabrics to endpapers for books.*

65–68 *These mid-19th-century English designs all draw their inspiration from high-quality contemporary Chinese ceramics which had been plundered from public buildings during the Ti-Ping Opium War rebellions. These pieces were very different from items made solely for export, which up to that time had accounted for nearly all of the Chinese objects collected in Europe and America. English designers found them to be "truly harmonious in colour and form." Many of these Chinese designs were quickly born again as English tiles, furnishings, and wallpapers. When we now see motifs and patterns of this type we don't immediately think of them as being Chinese; rather, we tend to regard them as prime examples of 19th-century English design—imagery that we associate with Victorian designers such as William Morris.*

65

67

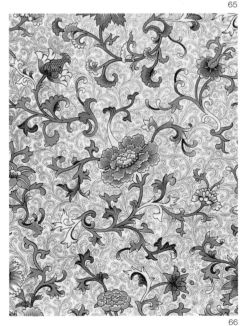

66

68

East Asia
China 4

69 Plum and willow trees, pagodas, figures in traditional Chinese dress crossing a bridge—these are all elements of what came to be known as "willow pattern." This 19th-century English textile takes its inspiration from earlier Chinese patterns and motifs. With its stylized imagery, drawn in the Western manner, it is a typical example of "chinoiserie."

70 This English frieze pattern, drawn in the middle of the 19th century, was inspired by the decoration on an early 19th-century Chinese bottle. In England, patterns of this type came to be used generally on wallpapers and pottery.

71 Two classic Chinese motifs, the phoenix and the cloud, provided the inspiration for this 19th-century textile. Probably French in origin, the cloth comprises embroidery on a woven ground. If you look closely you will see that the mazelike background pattern is made of interlocking swastikas, another Chinese motif.

69

70

71

72

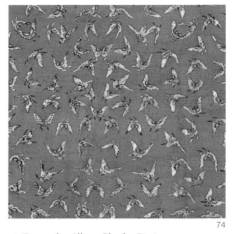

74

72 *Drawn by Albert Charles Racinet in the early 1870s, this pattern takes its inspiration from a Chinese fabric. While the six-pointed flower motif has been so heavily stylized that it is barely recognizable as Chinese, the underlying pattern of interlocking swastikas is beautifully drawn. The colors and the arrangement of motifs suggest that the fabric was possibly part of the lining of a robe or jacket.*

73 *This pattern has been taken from a large Chinese jar executed in cloisonné enamel. The technique involves soldering thin metal wires or strips onto a copper base to form little pockets. When these pockets are filled with glaze or enamel and fired, the colors melt to form brilliant ponds of color.*

74 *A mass of stylized butterflies— symbols of wedded bliss—are worked in gilt-thread tapestry upon a finely woven pale blue silk ground. The pattern decorates a 19th-century woman's garment, possibly a costly semiformal robe.*

73

East Asia
China 5

75

77

79

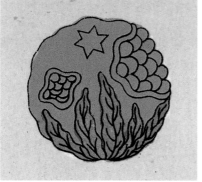
76

78

80

75–83 *Nine illustrations by Owen Jones, taking details and motifs directly from fine Chinese porcelain. Brilliantly colored Chinese pieces attracted particular attention in the West at the Great London Exhibitions of 1851 and 1855; the details here were published in Jones's book* The Grammar of Ornament *in 1856. Although the more basic blue-and-white Chinese wares had long been familiar to Western audiences, the forms of Chinese art were not widely understood and were crudely and unsympathetically imitated on cheap china throughout Europe. The designs here include a pomegranate, symbolic of fertility, and in Chinese art nearly always shown partially open to reveal its seeds; the lotus, an emblem of purity and one of the "eight treasures" of Buddhism, held in particular reverence in China; and a relatively naturalistic interpretation of the double gourd, a motif that often appears in a more formalized shape to symbolize the pairing of heaven and*

81

82

84

83

85

84 *Known as "Kaminari" (the Japanese word meaning thunderbolts), this motif is taken from a Chinese vase dating to the Heian period—the Japanese historical era 794–1185, when there were active trade relations between Japan and China. The square eddy in the form of a border indicates a thunderbolt, which in turn symbolizes strength and power.*

85 *This particular design is made up of a whole number of propitious symbols. Within the diamonds that encircle the royal flower, there are arranged and complete swastikas (a Buddhist symbol or mark of good fortune denoting happiness, benevolence, or an act of charity). Every part of the design is conveying messages that carry a symbolic strengthening of well-being.*

earth. The motifs are beautifully rendered and the colors are clean, bright, pure, and delicate. Even Jones, who was surprisingly not a fervent admirer of Chinese art, admitted that "the Chinese are certainly colourists, and are able to balance with equal success both the fullest tones of colour and the most delicate shades."